ROCKY MOUNTAIN HOME

ROCKY MOUNTAIN HOME

Spirited Western Hideaways

Elizabeth Clair Flood

Photographs by Peter Woloszynski

GIBBS·SMITH
P
PUBLISHER

SALT LAKE CITY

03 02 01 00 99   5 4 3 2 1

Published by

Gibbs Smith, Publisher

P.O. Box 667

Layton, Utah 84041

Website: *www.gibbs-smith.com*

Design by Kathy Timmerman, White Space Design Inferno

Cover design by Randall Smith Associates

Printed in Hong Kong

Library of Congress Cataloging-in-Publication Data

Rocky Mountain home : spirited western hideaways /

by Elizabeth Clair Flood : photography by Peter Woloszynski

p. cm.

ISBN 0-87905-704-1 (hb); ISBN 0-87905-904-4 (pbk)

1. Interior decoration—Rocky Mountains Region—History—20th century.

2. Decoration and ornament, Rustic—Rocky Mountains Region.

3. Interior decoration accessories—Rocky Mountains Region.

I. Woloszynski, Peter. II. Title.

NK2004.F66   1996

747'.9—dc20

95-47413

CIP

For Thomas, who always believed in this book

Contents

Preface

BACK WHEN MY LEGS were short and stuck out over my mother's chintz chair, living in a log cabin topped my fantasy list. I got this idea from an artist who lived in a pine forest at the top of Old La Honda Road in Woodside, California. She was by far my mother's most interesting friend. On our occasional visits to her cabin, I ran through the house barefoot along with her daughter, son, chickens, and dogs. We played her conga drums in the living room and rode her horses in the backyard. In the kitchen, bridles hung on the wall, colorful Fiesta cups and saucers cluttered the shelves, erotic postcards stuck to the fridge, and Hallmark cards and balloons dangled festively over an old, shiny blue wood-burning stove. Upstairs, white linens were wrinkly and unmade on a wrought-iron bed. I loved the mess. The brilliant clutter was the antithesis of our well-groomed city house. Here I could romp and not be scolded for tracking mud across mom's Sister Parish rugs.

A worn-out Old Hickory chair sits on the porch of an old dude cabin once located on the Valley Ranch in Cody, Wyoming. The cabin, with half-log siding typical of early cowboy architecture, has been moved to Wapiti, Wyoming, and is now a temporary home for guests.

Some twenty years later, I was looking at a cabin with a red door, a porch swing, and a great stone fireplace in Wilson, Wyoming. I knew I'd found my home. I couldn't wait to sit by a crackling

fire and drink coffee and watch snowflakes chase each other to the ground. During a major snowstorm, I'd happily bury myself under a quilt. And then, when night fell, leaving my cabin deliciously quiet and private, I would grab my sweetheart and two-step in the kitchen to the lively flicker of candlelight.

In winter, a cast-iron tub is a splendid refuge. A few small treasures—an early Yellowstone print, a squirrel candleholder, and a tin pitcher—spice up this simple 1950s bathroom. The floor is covered with practically indestructible sheet linoleum.

Friends and family seemed to understand. Treating my cabin fancy like an old-fashioned barn raising, they dropped off homemade furniture, lard cans full of wildflowers, and cassette tapes of cowgirl music. Pleased with my unconventional lifestyle, I truly believed I'd never file another complaint.

Sometime after I'd moved into my cabin, I was busy dusting cobwebs, stoking the stove, and trying to convince the neighborhood cat to stop drooling on my computer, when the phone rang. A gentleman named Peter with a British accent and a last name I didn't catch claimed he was a photographer for *The World of Interiors* and other European and American design magazines. He was in Jackson

A 1920s Old Hickory rocker, and a 1930s Thomas Molesworth club chair uphol-stered in Chimayo weavings from northern New Mexico provide comfortable places to relax in front of this stone fireplace. An old sleigh makes a good surface for tired feet.

Hole on vacation but was interested in shooting a few homes. Did I know of any suitable places? Would I meet him at the brew pub for a drink?

Now, I believe in good fortune, but this was most certainly a hoax. When I started writing

Western-style clothing
from the 1930s–'50s
—a riding skirt, some shirts,
ties, and a vest featuring
Buffalo Bill—work equally
well in this setting
as decoration.

about western homes and styling these places for regional magazines and for my first book, my mother had given me three copies of *The World of Interiors* from her own collection. She suggested that I try to emulate the magazine's styling techniques. The publication was considered by people in the business, worldwide, to be one of the definitive design magazines. Creating interiors like theirs proved a daunting task and remained a goal to which I aspired but felt hopelessly incapable of reaching. My rooms never had a spare, chic look about them; my towels never hung or folded smartly. Still suspicious of this international photographer, I agreed to meet him. Anything was more exciting than another evening with a drooling cat.

A bench built by Milo Marks of Texas and two 1940s spindle-back Old Hickory chairs surround a rustic kitchen table. A charming chicken sits atop a country cupboard.

As I walked into the pub, I recognized Peter wearing blue jeans, penny loafers, and a shocking yellow parka. We shook hands, exchanged pleasantries, and I told him I was working on another design book but didn't have a proper photographer. He said, "I'll do it." Going along with the joke, I laughed and said, "OK, great, when can you do it?" He said he would return to Jackson in one month, after a short assignment in Haiti. I hadn't even sipped my beer. The next day, I called my publisher to tell him we could move forward on our original book idea. I had found a photographer.

Despite my nagging, sleep-depriving fears that Peter wasn't really a professional and that the book deal, sealed over a Snake River Pale Ale, was just a good line, he arrived right on schedule, in a snowstorm, wearing his yellow jacket and carrying his cameras.

An elk with a deformed
rack holds court over this
1912 sunporch. Precious
winter sunlight warms the
original shiplap siding.
Two wicker chairs feature
cushions covered in a French
fabric from Pierre Deux.
A Navajo pound rug, circa
1880s, covers the table.

Feeling slightly uneasy at our first shoot, I talked with great speed about this and that while he proceeded to clear out two-years' worth of clutter on a 1912 sunporch, then take a picture of what remained: a stack of wood, an ax, and two weathered wicker chairs. When I looked at the Polaroid, I started to breathe again. The image was beautiful. The owners were so thrilled with the room's bare bones, they carted the cast-off items to the attic.

And so, this is how this book began.

For the next seventeen days, Peter and I, seated in our four-wheel-drive Avis van, rambled across Wyoming and Montana's wind-blown sagebrush plains and snowy mountain passes, listening to our limited selection of country tapes. We searched out people, places, and interior styles that caught our fancy. We were drawn to older homes, restored homestead cabins, and newer buildings that were in keeping with a pioneer style. Inside these rustic retreats, we discovered a practical and informal interior style. As we delved deeper into our project, the original book idea was clearly forgotten in the wake of our discoveries.

Architect Jonathan L. Foote, who has been in the Rockies long enough to know, divides western homes into two categories: the showplace and the usin' place. In *Rocky Mountain Home*, we chose to showcase predominantly the usin' place. That's where we found the style—a style which is as good as any in the world, and one distinctly American.

Wapiti, Wyoming, thirty-two miles from the east entrance of Yellowstone National Park, is a tiny town that retains the spirit of the western frontier.

This classic Wyoming barn
was built by Mel Annis.
It housed fine horses
raised by the Rocking H
Ranch and provided a
spacious dance floor for
the barn warming in 1928.

A colorful array of rosettes
frayed by the wind represent
years of first-class equestrian
performances by the ranch
owner.

A Crystal textile, circa 1930, covers a table inside a 1923 ranch house. Captain's chairs surround the table, and a Thomas Molesworth lamp featuring a horse-head carving by Wallace sits in the windowsill. Two pet buffalo—Tom and Sara—loll in the field beyond.

A functional tack room was created inside this restored 1910 bunkhouse from the Bradford Ranch on the North Fork of the Shoshone River in Cody, Wyoming.

Built in the 1930s for a
park ranger, this cabin now
serves as headquarters for a
couple who make their living
guiding fly fishermen.
An eclectic interior style
complements the traditional
hand-peeled logs and
quarter-round chinking.
Beacon blankets hang over
a leather couch;
precious *junque* clutters
the mantle. Arts and Crafts
reproduction candlesticks
by United Crafts grace the
desk on the back wall.
The floor is covered with
easy-care grass matting.

Old Navajo blankets
are stacked on an
eighteenth-century
American settle in a
mudroom outfitted for
all seasons. Settles were
designed for practical
application: their high,
solid backs helped keep
drafts off the occupants
who were warming in
front of the fireplace.

Flour-sack curtains cover the window of this old dude-ranch cabin. A yard-long photo of a Buffalo Bill Wild West Show, 1910, is displayed on the shelf.

A Pioneer Style

ONE WEEK INTO OUR TRIP, Peter and I stood on an empty highway in a downpour photographing Morton, Wyoming, population five. An abandoned general store and hotel stood on the left, and an old ranch and an Episcopal church bordered the right. Before we had a chance to meet these five unique individuals, an enormous truck sped by, drenching us in a tidal wave of grimy freeway rain. Soaked, we sought shelter in our van and continued down the lonely highway, flanked by miles of sagebrush and gray showers.

I later learned that Morton was established at the turn of the century by Mr. Joy Morton, a relative of the Morton Salt family. He and a partner named Edward H. Powers started building a canal in 1939. The project was later taken over by the government. Then the Schencks from Iowa moved in and built a garage and a general store, where travelers always stopped for a soft drink, a candy bar, and to visit. As one regular remembers, "People just stopped there to break up the monotony and say hello." Now a family from Rock Springs, Wyoming, is making a go of the place, ranching, building horse buggies, and doing other odd jobs

to stay alive. As far as I can make out, the town population has either been below five or slightly above for the last seventy years.

As we sped out of Morton, Peter and I wondered what it is about this country that invites people to live in the middle of nowhere. And how do they endure winter, which can last up to nine long, grueling months? Wyoming homesteaders used to say, "If summer falls on a weekend, let's have a picnic," writes John McPhee in his book *Rising From the Plains*. In an equally matter-of-fact tone, my friend's grandfather, a Colorado native, once told him, "It takes a lot of sack to endure winter in the Rockies." Having survived six winters of stone-cold car seats and unsexy layers of polypropylene and wool, I still looked out across the lonely plains and wondered what it is that makes people tough it out.

Listening to Trisha Yearwood sing "nothing but a fairytale" for the hundredth time, we arrived at the Busted Ass Ranch in Pavillion. For several years I had passed this remote place on my way to and from Cody, Wyoming. I'd always wondered why the the ranch sign,

Seven-year-old Michael calls himself "a regular hand" because he helps feed the animals on his grandfather's ranch. He wants to grow up to be a cowboy like his own grandfather and own his own ranch. Here he stands in the ranch house doorway of the Busted Ass Ranch, which is two double-wide trailers joined together then improved with log siding.

privy, windmill, and tractor were painted Pepto-Bismol pink, but never had the nerve to knock and ask. Today was different. I was accompanied by a photographer who was willing to do just about anything for a good picture.

The outhouse provided the original plumbing on the ranch, which was homesteaded in 1930. Of course, there is now indoor plumbing.

The windmill on the Busted Ass Ranch helps the owners predict the weather. "If it blows from the northeast, we'll get dumped on with snow. If it blows from the southwest, then we know we'll get some warm weather," they said.

As soon as we pulled into the ranch, Peter shot off to photograph the pink privy, while I was left to knock on the door and find him an umbrella. A man appeared and in a very friendly voice invited me in for a cup of coffee. First, he uncovered an umbrella, which I gave to Peter; then we returned indoors to get warm. While I chitchatted with him and his wife over coffee, the story of the pink paint unfolded.

"When you're young, you have three wishes about who you want to be when you grow up: a fireman, a policeman, or a cowboy. And I always wanted to be a cowboy," said the man. Five years ago, he quit the fiberglass business in New Jersey and moved to Wyoming, our least-populated state. His wife was stunned when he said, "I'm gone," and walked out, and a few weeks later they were scouting the Cowboy State for "a secluded place with trees."

After scouring the sagebrush plains, the New Jersey couple stumbled onto their ranch, just outside Pavillion. They encased two double-wide trailers in log, then christened their home the Busted Ass Ranch. The man wanted to call it the Busting Ass Ranch, since they never stop working there, but his wife convinced him the past tense sounded better. For these city slickers, the Busted Ass Ranch—a log cabin, a barn full of animals that have become their pets, some hay fields, a quiet, friendly neighborhood nearby—was a dream come true. Even though living was tough, they would endure just about anything to stay. Returning to New Jersey was out of the question.

And the pink? Left alone one weekend, the husband trimmed the cabin and other outbuildings with a homemade concoction of red and white. When his wife returned, she stared with dismay. After much discussion, she reached into her pocket, pulled out a bright pink Bic lighter, and suggested that even *this* color would be more appropriate. To her surprise, her husband was game, and they headed down to Wal-Mart and purchased thirty gallons of bright pink. Like tossing tinsel on a fir tree, they celebrated their good fortune by painting not only their ranch sign this lovely shade of pink but also the barn doors, outhouse, gate, and tractor. The husband even invested in a pair of handmade burgundy chaps, burgundy suspenders, and a pink button-down shirt. To the whole town's delight, he sports his pink attire and rides his pink tractor in the local homecoming parade.

When I asked if he owned a pink hat, he turned to me with an absolutely straight face. "No, I will not wear a pink cowboy hat. I have to draw the line somewheres."

For everyone, that line is in a different place. But it was in the spirit of the Busted Ass Ranch that many people moved west. Most Rocky Mountain homes provided a hearth for settlers in search of a more fulfilling life. Scattered over a vast frontier, the log cabin—the most practical building at the time—emerged as a symbol of hope, opportunity, and a healthy change of pace. An interior style naturally

Although no longer in use, this hand-hewn, early-twentieth-century church is an essential element in a western landscape. Old buildings like this one connect us to our history and are meaningful reminders of our ancestors who worked hard and took risks to forge a life in the wilderness.

evolved from the materials at hand. For those building "log castles" in the sky, as one pioneer gal called her homestead dream, tales of hardship fell on deaf ears. Rocky Mountain pioneers soon learned to swill and swallow the bittersweet.

The first non-Native American people to move into the Rockies were trappers, bachelors, thieves or men on the dodge, and hunters coveting their own private hunting grounds. They built one-room cabins far from civilization. In most cases these mountain men had only the bare minimum of necessities: a stove, a bed tick filled with straw, and a few pieces of crude, handmade furniture. As these dyed-in-the-wool westerners settled into their soogans, or blankets, wind beat at the front door and snow hissed through the cabin chinking. Despite severe conditions, they endured. The thrill of adventure, the luxury of independence, the promise of solitude, and the drama of the landscape made this wild country the object of desire.

Soon others recognized opportunity in this country inhabited by boot-leather-tough individuals. Old-timers called this opportunity "elbow room." When Congress announced the Homestead Act of 1862, offering free land, few people needed prodding. Thousands of folks quickly packed their belongings, gathered their

A couple from Bondurant, Wyoming, prepare meals and heat their cabin with this old Banquet restaurant stove from the Great Western Stove Company. The stove, patented in 1898, was installed in the cabin in 1920, when the place was a dude ranch. Bringing a pot of cold water to a boil on the stove takes from forty-five minutes to an hour—a sure way to help a person slow down. Although the owners are slaves to the stove all winter, the lady of the house says, "The heat tickles you to death when the electricity goes out and it's forty below outside."

A portrait of a turn-of-the-century Montana pioneer decorates a small powder room at the Mangy Moose Saloon in Jackson Hole. The walls have been papered with *National Geographic* maps.

stock, loaded their families in ox-driven wagons, and headed west of the Mississippi River, across what was called The Great American Desert, to establish roots on the hundreds of thousands of unappropriated public acres. Designed to encourage small, independent farmers and ranchers—not developers—to settle the frontier, the Homestead Act offered settlers 160-acre parcels. To gain ownership of the land, claimants were required to live on the property for at least six months every year for a five-year period and make improvements, including a twelve-by-twelve cabin. The most successful homesteads were built next to water. Sagebrush flats indicated fertile ground.

This country schoolhouse was built at the turn of the century on Montana's East Boulder River and was closed down in 1962. Builder Terry Baird is helping the Boe Ranch Company of McLeod, Montana, restore the building. Once finished, it will be rented out as a summer guest cottage.

In 1914, rodeo star Vera McGinnis dreamed of settling down on a ranch with her husband, Earl Simpson. Pierce Cunningham, her friend and one of the first to put down roots in Jackson Hole, insisted she and her sweetheart try his neck of the woods. "Come on home with me and spend the winter. There's lots of open homestead land, good feed the year round, good hunting and fishing. Golly whack, there's no other place like it."

Convinced, the couple packed up their horses and belongings and trailed over Teton Pass, an eight-thousand-foot divide, into Jackson Hole, where they discovered little log cabins with smoke rolling out the chimneys. In her book *Rodeo Road*, Vera wrote, "Ever since I'd left my office job to ride in my first rodeo at Salt Lake City I'd been driving

myself. Hurrying to get from one show to the next, hurrying to the hotels, hurrying to the show grounds, hurrying horses here and hurrying horses there. It now dawned on me that I was fed up with hurry. It felt good to be headed for the sticks, in no rush about anything, with rodeos the least of my worries or cares." Furthermore, "Pioneering just fits my pistola," she said to Earl.

En route to her future home, Vera soaked up the peace and quiet in the air, admired the rugged, wild beauty, and dreamed of her three-room log cabin. "We'd hew the logs and face it toward the Teton Peaks. . . ."

When the couple arrived, winter was already well on its way, so they didn't have time to stake out their 160 acres or construct a twelve-by-twelve cabin. Instead, they moved into an old, dilapidated but uninhabited cabin near the Cunninghams. This particular cabin had been used for years as a camp for hunters, drifting cowboys, and shady characters on the move. It was a three-room cabin joined with the saddle-notched joints. In keeping with tradition, the previous owners probably stuffed matts of horsehair and cow pies between the logs, then nailed quarter-round chinking—slats of wood—over the crude insulation. The roof was made of poles, then packed with dirt, which is the reason why these cabins were nicknamed soddies.

Crude log-and-board furniture and an old cookstove give character to this modernized homestead kitchen. Cream cans, circa 1910, help keep the spirit of the original homesteaders present in the decor.

After Earl returned from the main town some forty miles away with a wagon load of supplies, Vera went about creating a comfortable home with what she had. Relying on lye, hot water, and perseverance, she turned the old floor into a smooth thing of beauty. Then, from a bolt of red-and-white-checked oilcloth, she cut a tablecloth and a worktable cover, then lined the numerous warped one-by-twelve shelves. With Earl's help, she tacked cheesecloth onto the ceiling to prevent the dirt from falling on their heads. She placed a borrowed rag carpet on the floor, polished the rusty stove, and bleached and sewed flour sacks into functional and attractive cabinet doors. A straw-tick bunk covered in Navajo blankets provided a suitable couch. With extra fabric scraps and straw stuffing, she made pillows. After restuffing the bed tick with straw and filling the kerosene lamp, Vera surveyed the cozy place with pride. The home looked great, despite the fact that a carpet-slung rocker was the only store-bought piece of furniture in the whole place. Like many western decorators before her and many after, Vera created a warm and informal environment.

"When Earl came home, even he noticed; he whistled, 'Whew! Pretty slick for this neck of the woods, if you ask me.' Then he grabbed me and waltzed me around and around the room. I felt well repaid for my effort.

"Now we're ready for company," Vera said.

He grinned and shook his head. "Don't feel bad if nobody comes for a while."

Sadly, barns like this
one that have deteriorated
over the years have been
burned down to decrease
property taxes. More
and more, however, builders
and architects are
interceding and buying up
the old structures to
reuse the precious weathered
wood. The old wood,
distressed by wind, snow,
and sun, gives new buildings
history and some soul
that new materials just
can't provide.

An early homestead cabin, now a guest house, features a 1930s hand-hewn sideboard and chair by Wesley Bircher of Wilson, Wyoming. In keeping with the vintage furniture, a 1920s Two Grey Hills Navajo rug covers the original wood floor. The buffalo skull was uncovered from a bog nearby—a poignant reminder that life in the Rockies is intimately connected to the frontier.

Snowbound

WINTER IS NEVER FAR from the Rocky Mountains. As early as August, cold air descends from snowcapped peaks and steals down the canyons, making animals and barefoot-and-suntanned inhabitants shuffle restlessly. Some greet the turn in temperature with delight; others grumble but diligently prepare for a snow-covered world. A few droop in despair like frost-bitten dahlias and abandon the high country.

Every year I'm overwhelmed with winter preparations. For many residents the cycle is old hat. Crisp fall air rings in the pika's ears like an alarm clock, signaling the time to build grass haystacks for winter pantries. Squirrels stash food in bottomless cheeks as trout spawn in the chilly, dark waters and beavers hurry to reinforce their river hideouts. Nearby, the neighborhood cat mews loudly in search of food and a warm place to stay over the next six months. Without much ado, grizzlies slip off into their dens for a winter siesta.

With the same urgency and habit as birds flocking for migration, cowboys harvest the hay fields for winter feed and herd cattle from the high country to the lowlands.

In the spring and summer, this sod-roofed cabin—once the home of a pioneer family—is used as a small garden house. Wildflowers grow on the roof.

In this cabin redesigned by
architect Jonathan Foote,
windows frame the outdoors.
The owner enjoys close-up
views of the woods as well
as long-distance vistas of
the Teton Mountain Range.

Experienced settlers busy themselves getting meat in the freezer. Ski bums gather and split wood, stock cabinets with hot cocoa, upgrade equipment, adjust snow tires and chains, plastic-coat their windows, and happily slip into long underwear and wool socks.

When the bull elk's high-pitched bugle echoes through glowing red-and-yellow cottonwood trees, announcing rutting season, summer dudes and dudeens who don't wish to be a part of the chosen frozen pack their belongings and depart for warmer climes. As the skiers discuss the *Farmer's Almanac*'s snowfall predictions, I insist on wearing summer T-shirts and sandals and drinking lemonade until snow buries the last scrub of sagebrush.

During the winter, however, a rich, cozy life unfolds around the hearth. Pioneers found that a small, hand-hewn cabin with a low ceiling and human-scale rooms provided a safe, manageable refuge from miles and miles of cold and ice and below-fifty temperatures. One stove usually heated the entire cabin. Few would have built a larger house, given the opportunity. A larger home required more firewood, and with fields to harvest, livestock to tend, and winter pantries to be stocked, there just wasn't time to support a larger house.

Today, there is something romantic about the scale of these old cabins that invites a person inside when the wind is howling and a snowstorm is raging. Heat from a stove draws a person to a hearth.

Snow piles up outside French doors that were added to the upstairs bedroom of this homestead cabin.

Once a Montana homestead, this 1890 cabin, restored by architect Jonathan Foote, now sits in a Wyoming aspen grove. It is 20 by 38 feet, with dovetail joints. "I like the home's age," says the homeowner. "It has a spirit that new homes lack."

The rustic texture of the walls and floors in these primitive hideouts are pleasing to the eye and the touch. One feels like an adventurer. Never mind that the old-timer down the block who grew up in a one-room homestead cabin nearby now lives in a snug

A barn-wood wall with wood-and-rawhide snowshoes in the alcove are an indoor reminder of the land that lies beyond the cabin walls.

frame house. Over coffee one morning he told me he wouldn't dream of living in a log cabin in this severe climate. "Dudes live in log cabins. We know better." Another Wyoming lady, who called herself a "homestead brat," grew up in cabins but now also lives in a nice frame house. "Well, I'll tell you, I got tired of the log cabins," she said. "Every crack had air coming through it." They did serve a purpose at the time, she admits. "They were nicer than the dugouts some people lived in."

ONE OF THE GREATEST TRADITIONS to evolve from winter living was the proliferation of rustic pole furniture. Similar to other rustic traditions across the world, ordinary folks built their own furniture because they needed it, and long winter hours gave them the time.

Most of this rustic furniture developed in remote areas where

The colors and textures of Navajo blankets give this room a warm aura, even on the coldest of days. The wall art is by cowboy artist Charlie Dye of Canyon City, Colorado (1906–1972).

machine-made furniture was inaccessible, which would explain why there isn't much pole furniture in more civilized areas of Montana, Colorado, Wyoming, and Idaho.

Log-home builder and furniture maker
Wesley Bircher of Wilson, Wyoming,
spent hours trying to find matching
curved branches to frame the sides of
this lodgepole desk he built in the
1930s. "I did my homework on this
desk as a boy growing up," said
Bircher's grandson, who also has the
matching bed and dresser.

A 1930s chest built by Cliff Clark
of Seely Lake, Montana, occupies an
old cabin. The geometric applied-pole
design resembles work fashioned in
the Adirondacks some fifty years
before. The drawers for this piece were
made from used ammunition boxes.

Clyde Anderson of Billings, Montana,
built this rustic table and chairs
in 1930. The new owners say it is
"surprisingly comfortable."

Since straight lodgepole pine was plentiful in the northern Rockies, most of the early furniture pieces were made of pine. Some were fashioned from moose, elk, and deer antlers. One Montana craftsman, hard-pressed for material, used the wood from old ammunition boxes to make the drawers for a small pole chest.

The popularity of dude ranches in the early part of this century spurred the creation of better-crafted lodgepole furniture much as the population of the Adirondacks by wealthy people encouraged local craftsmen to build fine furniture there. To provide a comfortable and western experience for well-to-do eastern travelers—nurtured on romantic dime novels and pulp fiction—ranchers needed suitable beds, tables, chairs, and couches. To fulfill their expectations, experienced woodworkers created burled beds, bureaus overlaid with half-poles and antler pulls, and fanciful furniture inspired by a twist of wood. Many of the pieces reflected meticulous craftsmanship and unusual detail. Pine cones were used for pulls; antler ashtrays were incorporated into a settee; preserved animal legs were often used to support a table, lamp, or ashtray.

Men such as Albert W. Gabby of Jackson Hole, Wyoming, and E. Rathe of Montana built some of the earliest pole furniture for ranches circa 1920. Gabby created geometric patterns with applied pole much like the Adirondack craftsmen did. Rathe used burled wood to create exquisitely balanced pieces. Bob and Jack Kranenberg; brothers Albert,

Dude-ranch cabins like these provided a cozy escape for western travelers in the early part of this century. Residing in a small cabin in the Rockies is still a romantic longing.

Charlie, Otto, and Neal Nelson; and Wesley Bircher provided furniture for Jackson Hole ranches and dude cabins in the twenties, thirties, and forties. John Wertz built elegant antler furniture and Bill Green built pole furniture into the forties and fifties. At the same time, others, such as O. C. Houchin and Clyde Anderson of Billings and Cliff Clark of the Seely Lake area, were building rustic furniture in Montana. Of course, Thomas Molesworth started building rustic furniture in the thirties in Cody, Wyoming, inspiring more craftsmen such as Paul and Don Hindman, Pete Fritjofson, Ralph Knight, and George Blackford.

A strong rustic furniture tradition continues today in the Rocky Mountains. Wyoming native Mike Wilson builds antler furniture, chandeliers, and sconces because his family always did. He grew up living with his great-uncle Kid Wilson at his Sweetwater Lodge in Cody. As a boy, Mike trailed behind his elders when they went hunting or sat by their side when they stayed home on a snowy day tying flies, building fishing rods and guns, and creating antler doorknobs, knife handles, gate latches, furniture, and trinkets. "My uncle never threw antler away. Making things was something he did to keep himself busy in the winter."

A chandelier called the Wyoming Sunrise, built by Mike Wilson, hangs in a homestead cabin that is now used as a guest house. A ticking blanket covers the bed. Both the bed and the dresser were built by Wesley Bircher of Wilson, Wyoming, in the thirties. A framed 1920s advertisement is a kitschy addition to this rustic room.

A moose head with a five-foot rack holds court over John and Pam Mortensen's living room. The eclectic interior showcases a blend of rustic western furniture, Indian and Persian rugs, and John's own sculpture and chair. Johnny Wertz's antler settee, built in Hoback, Wyoming, circa 1920, is a rare find. The handmade lodgepole desk from Pam's family dude ranch—the GP Bar in the Wind River Mountains—is believed to have been built by W. B. "Doc" Rickert, a Forest Service ranger in Kendall, Wyoming. An early Teec Nos Pas rug, also from the GP Bar, hangs behind the settee.

Wilson also learned from Jackson Hole antler craftsman and log-home builder Otto Nelson. Despite the wretched smell of rotting buffalo skins in the corner of Nelson's cabin, Wilson hung around to learn something about the elder's craft.

"Old-timers were perfectionists, and I think one of the reasons they were perfectionists was just because they had the time to be that way."

By continuing to be an outfitter and a fine antler craftsman, Wilson carries on a family legacy. More than an art, his work is a way of life. "I don't just build antler furniture," he says, tucking a plug of Red Man tobacco in his cheek. "I'm into living a Wyoming lifestyle and I am very serious about it. Yeah, I have a fax machine, but I hunt and butcher all my own game, I make my own jerky, and I put up my own food." After chatting with Mike, he sent me down the road with a hunk of elk meat and a recipe for elk stew, which didn't turn out half bad.

This Bondurant, Wyoming, cabin and all its furnishings were made by homesteader Bill Sargent in 1937. Following in his footsteps, the present owner, Becky Lacina, constructed the willow chair. Her husband Rik's beer-can collection is displayed in the background.

ALTHOUGH BUILDING FURNITURE helped pass the winter for some, the long snow season was unquestionably grueling. As Vera's cowboy said, "[Homesteading is] nothin' but work, buckin' the weather, skimpin', savin', and doin' without." For the most part, families buried in cabins laden with snow found the winters lonely and cold. There was illness and death. People waited months for a letter to arrive via horseback or snowshoe. And bachelors subscribed to the Heart and Hand Club in hopes of finding a lady companion.

Writer Donald Hough reports that many Jackson Hole cowboys drowned their winter sorrows in créme de menthe. Every summer, cowboys fell in love with beautiful dude girls from the East, who drank this Madison Avenue cocktail in such wild 'n' wooly places as the Million Dollar Cowboy Bar. For the most part, the debutantes promised to love these roughnecks forever; but most likely, once the girls crossed the Continental Divide, all a cowboy could expect was a picture postcard of the Empire State Building—if that. With luck, by midwinter and after an uncountable number of green drinks, a cowboy usually bucked his loneliness and met a western gal who, as Hough attests, "nine times out of ten, was a better woman."

One cowboy on winter ranch duty tempered his cabin fever by reading the magazines plastering the walls—a pioneer solution for wallpaper—until the spring roundup. Some people weren't cured that easily. After being cooped up all winter, Miss Waxham, a Wyoming schoolteacher, wrote in her journal, "My spirit has a chair sore."

Winter tests people's ability to survive.

One evening in 1873, an English traveler named Isabella Bird spent the night in a one-room cabin in Estes Park, Colorado, and

A mission-style couch and a wooden trunk occupy the center of this Montana homestead cabin, restored by Terry Baird and decorated by Hilary Heminway. As in early cabins, the hearth, sitting room, kitchen, and dining room are all located in a single small room. An upstairs level was added during remodeling.

discovered that cabins aren't always adequate shelter in a severe winter storm. "I had gone to sleep with six blankets on, and a heavy sheet over my face," she wrote in her book, *A Lady's Life in the Rocky Mountains*. "Between two and three [a.m.] I was awoke by the cabin being shifted from underneath by the wind, and the sheet was frozen to my lips. I put out my hands, and the bed was thickly covered with fine snow. Getting up to investigate matters, I found the floor some inches deep in parts in fine snow, and a gust of fine, needle-like snow stung my face. The bucket of water was solid ice. I lay in bed freezing till sunrise, when some of the men came to see if I 'was alive' and 'to dig me out.'"

Like other diehards, however, Isabella was undaunted by the experience and returned to the mountains in winter on several occasions. Addicted to the intoxicating air, she muddled through the more difficult times. Despite the cold, she enjoyed the peace and simplicity of the cabin.

"I *really* need nothing more than this log cabin offers," she wrote. "But elsewhere one must have a house and servants, and burdens and worries. . . . My log house takes me about five minutes to 'do,' and you could eat off the floor, and it needs no lock, as it contains nothing worth stealing."

An English armoir, circa 1850, holds a collection of Pendleton blankets and Indian textiles. Willow chairs, which are used both indoors and outdoors, are a traditional accent to a western home.

MacDuff Thane of Fief VII
trots through the snow to a
hand-hewn turn-of-the-
century cabin, moved from
Yellowstone National Park to
a location near Jackson.

WHILE CABIN FEVER RUNS rampant in these parts, the grim malady doesn't stop the fancies of cabin romantics. My neighbor has a turn-of-the-century Yellowstone cabin at the far end of her property. "Fixed up a little, it could be a great little escape," she said. "Escape from what, I don't know." Curious, Peter and I strapped into old snowshoes. He carried the camera, I toted the knapsack packed with lunch: a bottle of Blandy's port, salami, and fresh bread from the local pâtisserie. MacDuff Thane of Fief VII, a Scotty who was been known to nip on occasion, eagerly led the way.

Progress into the woods was slow. As we trudged through deep snow and serpentine pine trees, I kept tripping over my large webbed feet, landing in the most unusual positions. When we finally neared the weather-beaten cabin, MacDuff gloated in the crooked doorway.

We stepped inside to discover the place was empty. Some cowboy's initials marked a weathered beam. Glassless windows framed a Never-Never-Land winter in all directions. Spying a mountain bluebird balanced on a pine bough, I imagined fixing up the cabin with a wood-burning stove and a rocking chair; then, on a snowy day, when no one was looking, I would steal up here on my reliable cross-country skies and indulge in the solace and isolation.

Peter interrupted my daydream, reminding me of our next appointment. We left reluctantly, hiking out with the same amount of difficulty—and laughter.

A deserted cabin is an ideal setting for a winter picnic and provides respite from the strenuous activity of snowshoeing.

Probably built in the 1920s, the Watercress Cabin in Wilson, Wyoming, has captured a number of buyers' fancy, but the owner reserves the romantic space for his guests.

When Bruce Simon first moved to Jackson Hole, he lived in this 1930s cabin for $75 a month. After a few years, the owner agreed to sell it to him for $750—$400 for the cabin and $350 for the contents. Simon moved the cabin from town to a wooded area, where he lived without electricity and modern plumbing for a year, just to see what it would be like. After modernizing the place, adding an upstairs bedroom, and tacking up the old ranger-station sign, he decided to rent the home. The porch chair is made of antlers—a renewable resource in the Rockies.

By surrounding the upstairs bedroom with four windows, Simon created a magical space. From a cozy bed, occupants view a forest all around them. "I just wanted to bring the outdoors in," says Simon. The bed is covered with a Navajo Transitional weaving, Germantown 1880s. It was once a man's wearing blanket. An early-nineteenth-century folk-art weathervane finds a new use as a room sculpture.

A farm table looks just right
in this 1930s ranger cabin.
Cut flowers or forced blooms
are a wonderful remedy for
cabin fever.

A *buffet a deux corts*,
circa 1825, makes a
stunning entry piece in
this 1930s cabin.

Disappearing into a small cabin in the woods in winter gives me goose bumps. It's not that I dream of being a solitary recluse like Thoreau or boasting about my cabin in a presidential campaign like Abe Lincoln and many other U.S. presidents. It's simply the thrill of escape. Snow falling outside a rough-hewn window mysteriously invites me to abandon routine.

I'm not alone in these feelings. There is a small three-room homestead cabin up the road from me, where I often imagine myself snowbound. To my surprise, everyone to whom I mention this place melts into his or her own giddy, romantic notions about holing up in the same retreat. Like the desperadoes of the Hole-in-the-Wall Gang discovered, there is no better place to hide out than in the Rockies in winter when the sun sets early, drawing a curtain of darkness around the country and one's abode.

Up a short flight of stairs in an old 1930s cabin, a gal who created a successful flower shop in town sleeps in a square bedroom, surrounded by four windows. In the winter, the small bedroom glows like a lighthouse, casting a seductive warmth over a sea of snowy treetops. Throughout the season, snow falls off the roof, creating a step stool for mangy moose, who climb right up to the window to nibble the branches off an aspen tree. Some press their long "Gerard Depardieu noses," as Peter calls them, up against the glass.

"The room feels so separate from the house. I can't even see any other homes through the windows. I feel like I am in an entirely different place." On a full-moon night, she can read without a lamp. On typically chilly mornings, like forty below, she finds it difficult to extract herself from the covers. "Sometimes I stay up there all day." Originally from Georgia, my friend moved to Jackson to enjoy winter sports, escape city crowds, and start her own business. Like her lighthouse bedroom, the small mountain town of Jackson makes her feel safe and self-sustaining, even though a storm is threatening.

Bubba, a curious Maine coon, keeps a lookout from the top of a country cabinet.

This cozy bedroom inside
a Jonathan Foote home
features a rustic bed from
Vermont covered in a
Beacon-style blanket. The
large white cabinet with
a hinged door resembling
a barn door provides a
spacious closet.

Simply styled bathroom
fixtures complement the
recycled timber used by
architect Jonathan Foote.

A feminine bedstead and
linens juxtapose brilliantly
against the rough-hewn
walls of this rustic home.

A backbone found on a Wyoming
trail is a simple decoration on this dresser,
created to look old.

A Third Phase Transitional Chief's
blanket, circa 1885, hangs over this
bedroom fireplace.

The owners of this turn-of-the-
century moose traded three Navajo rugs
for the head. An 1890 Chief's
blanket hangs below.

In this modern Wyoming ski house,
designer Astrid Sommer creates a comfortable
ambience with a Molesworth chair and a
couch upholstered in Chimayo weavings, textiles
from northern New Mexico. The coffee table is
an old cobbler's bench. Flour-sack pillows
make the chairs comfy.

This home, designed by
Imaging Spence and built by
Jackson contractor Michael
Beauchemin, combines
native materials and an
Old World imagination.
"I designed it on a cocktail
napkin and then made
models out of boxes and
Lincoln Logs," Spence says.

A viable option to building a new retreat is to turn an empty, weathered building like this into a private office, a charming guest house, or a playhouse.

Early fishing gear—bamboo rods, wicker creels, and an old minnow can—make rich decorative accessories in the Rocky Mountains, where fly-fishing has become all the rage. Vintage sporting gear can be found in most western antique and junk shops.

Old Hickory furniture, circa 1930, and a primitive cowboy chair furnish the sunporch of a 1923 Wyoming ranch house, which can be comfortable even in winter.

Hideouts

THREADING THE NORTHERN Rockies, Peter and I continued to alight on people enjoying cozy retreats like the girl in the lighthouse room. We were delighted to discover that not everyone was building megahomes, or "log cabins on steroids," to steal a phrase from a longtime resident at my neighborhood potluck.

This new Montana soddy was designed to "look" like it has been around a hundred years. With logs from Montana's Flying D Ranch, architect David Leavengood and Yellowstone Traditions recreated this primitive shelter for modern use. Instead of using mortar, the chinking is a synthetic material applied dry to create a rough, hand-troweled appearance. This method is practical, because the synthetic material expands and contracts with the logs and doesn't crack. It also provides better insulation than the traditional quarter-round or cement chinking. The cabin is joined with saddle notches, and the tips of the logs are finished with chopper points, a style invented by pioneers using hand axes.

Rustic furniture, family quilts, old wood-burning stoves, outdoor laundry lines, and vintage coffeepots revealed a deep, pervading nostalgia for a simpler way of life. It was a surprise to discover that a well-known Hollywood star steals away to a restored three-room homestead cabin along a Montana creek. A native ranch gal impressed me with her tale of living in a one-room cabin in Idaho. For several years, she lived without electricity and running water and cooked on an old Ashley stove, not because of some romantic notion, but because that's what she could afford at the time. In the evenings she lit candles,

Designed by Hilary Heminway, this soddy interior features an Old Hickory rocker and a diamond-willow bed and hat rack crafted by Diane Cole of Bozeman, Montana. Cole builds with diamond willow because the strong wood has plenty of character in its bark and branches. The Yellowstone sign above the fireplace is a modern piece. The cabin flooring is from an old blacksmith's shop, and the granite stone on the fireplace was collected from the surrounding area. The screen was hand forged by George Ainslie of Lavina, Montana, and the granite stone was quarried and hewed by Big Sky Masonry.

and when her pyramid of dirty dishes teetered on the counter, she washed the lot in her tub. "That was the simplest, most serene time in my life."

SITTING AT THE historic Irma Hotel in Cody, Wyoming, under the shadow of the Victorian cherry-wood backbar, circa 1902—a $100,000 present from the Queen of England to Buffalo Bill Cody—Peter and I tried to persuade a local couple to take us to their secret hideout. They seemed a bit reluctant. They rarely invited guests to their place. In the end, they agreed.

The next day, we traveled up Cody's rugged South Fork Valley along a paved road, then down a dirt road that passed through a herd of Herefords and an old dude ranch. Suddenly, our friend leapt out of the car and flagged down a man dressed in Carhartt coveralls and a plaid Elmer Fudd hat. He explained what we were doing and asked if we could have a peek inside his old place. "I remember they had a really great old fireplace in here," my friend said. As the screen door creaked open and slammed shut, we filed into a place that looked as if it hadn't changed in a hundred years. Chipped seafoam green paint— a color one Wyoming native affectionately called "grandma green," because in the thirties it was used on everything in Wyoming from sheep wagons to houses—coated the living-room wall. Bear traps, snowshoes, and lanterns decorated the dusty stone mantel. Two weathered Indiana sassafras chairs flanked the fireplace, and between them lay a bearskin rug; a few claws still hung from the paws. Come summer, the man explained, his ninety-one-year-old stepmother—who as a young gal had visited the area as a dude—will return to stay in this building, as she has done for many summers of her life.

Thrilled with this glimpse of the real thing, we thanked the owner, and continued down the dirt road, then broke trail across a sagebrush hill. After a while, we stopped and got out. Although there was snow on all the peaks around us, the wind had swept most of the snow from the valley. Down inside an arroyo stood the couple's ramshackle shed—the perfect hideout.

Ten years ago, he and his wife had built a lean-to and a fire pit on this same piece of land but closer to the river. Because the man worked for a furniture maker nearby, he used the place as a temporary residence while his wife and children lived closer to town. "After a couple of years, I got tired of cooking over a fire, so I built a toolshed," he said. Like an animal, he studied the lay of the land before building the home. "It was a really hard place to establish habitat, because where the river was and where the lean-to was, there was a wind tunnel. In the early spring, gravel flew three hundred feet in the air."

An Old Hickory table, two chairs, and a circa-1900 pie safe create an intimate dining area in this 1930s cabin.

This river-rock and fossil-rock fireplace welcomed travelers far and wide to the Irma Hotel in Cody, Wyoming, built in 1902 by Buffalo Bill Cody. For over ninety years, the Irma has been the gathering place for local stockmen, wool growers, and oilmen. Tens of thousands of dollars still change hands over a cup of coffee and a handshake.

Built with local river rock and petrified shells, this fireplace was the hearth for dudes visiting Sam Aldridge's dude ranch in the 1920s. The bearskin rug, traps, and Indiana sassafrass chairs from the same era were placed in the room by subsequent owners.

This Wyoming ranch house was built around 1900. Through the years, the owners added on to the original structure. The home is now one of the main ranch buildings for the Siggins Polled Hereford Ranch.

Looking down at the original lean-to site from the outlaw porch, he continued, "I was lucky to be able to cruise the area for a year and a half to two years to see where the weather came and how everything was. It's important to realize what's happening in an area before you site your place. You could really put your home in the wrong place in this country and make a big mistake." They passed on one site because they believed a building would insult the natural beauty.

The present arroyo location, just above the creek, is out of the wind and up against a spring. Once or twice a month, the couple runs off to their shed for a break in routine and to enjoy each other's company. Like pioneers, they cook on a woodstove and light their modest space with a kerosene lamp. They find the simplicity of living with the bare necessities rejuvenating. And the quiet helps them put the rapidly spinning world in perspective. Of course, even these two splurge on a few luxuries, such as a gourmet lunch and a bottle of 1983 Bordeaux, which all of us enjoyed in this wild, romantic place. For a few hours, even we forgot where we were headed next.

Jimmy Covert gave the old cookstove—a Quick Meal circa 1930—to his wife for Mother's Day. The tilt-table chair, which turns into a table, was built by an old Montana cowboy. The piece was probably built for a one-room cowcamp where there wasn't room for furniture, Covert speculates. "It has the initials of the cowboy on it, a great patina, and wear signs." Pictures from *Western Horseman* magazine plaster the ceiling here as they did in many cowcamps of years past.

Handcrafted by Jimmy
Covert, this wine-tasting
table features a fir base and
a white oak top. The cherry-
wood table surface features
an inlay of grapevine.
An assortment of rustic
chairs surrounds the table.
Covert's own driftwood wind
chimes seem to spin magic
around this retreat.

In the South Fork Valley
outside Cody, Wyoming, this
ramshackle toolshed hideout,
decorated with logs hauled
out of the river, faces the
Absaroka Mountains. Owners
Jimmy and Lynda Covert,
who are practicing furniture
artists, spend many hours
here, enjoying the outdoors
and each other's company.
Because the hideout is
completely hidden from the
view of passersby, the
Coverts felt free to build it
just the way they wanted it,
without having to worry
what others might think.

BACK IN JACKSON HOLE, we met a California girl who moved to Wyoming because she wanted to live in a remote mountain community where everyone knew each other and didn't scowl when you asked to borrow an egg. For these reasons, she fell in love with Wilson, Wyoming, where she now lives full-time in her version of a lighthouse—a 260-square-foot trailer. Although she would like a little more room for an art studio and for her collection of Barbie dolls, plastic dinosaurs, and pink flamingos, she enjoys cozy winter days sitting in her armchair by the stove.

But having a small space wasn't enough. When her landlord wasn't looking, she painted her home-sweet-home to look like a log cabin, then created a jolly Elvis peeking out the window. "With all the log architecture in this area, it just seemed like the natural thing to do," she says. And Elvis? "He's just an Elvis thing." There was no need to fear the landlord's reaction to her one-room log cabin trailer. Like everyone else, she laughed, "I like it. It's fun."

Many log cabin dreams aren't quite so modest.

Torn between their family's desire for a small log cabin in the woods and their need for a large space, a longtime Wyoming resident designed a seventeen-room, log-and-stone cowboy castle in a Wyoming aspen grove. Inspired by the grandness of Yosemite's Ahwahnee, Yellowstone's Old Faithful Inn,

Every summer, artist Greta Gretzinger packs up her Mona-Lisa Subaru with tiger-striped seats and a gold-fringed window and tours the Rockies solo. It isn't difficult for her to meet people, she says. "Most people look at my car and smile. They take it as a friendly, open kind of thing." After sleeping in her car for three weeks, she looks forward to living in her trailer. "It feels so big. It has running water and a warm stove."

"My interior decor evolved because I'm a pack rat," Gretzinger says. She combs yard sales and the local thrift shop for treasures. She has to be careful not to fill the trailer too full, however, as she needs room to do her mixed-media work.

and an array of Scottish castles, the fairy-tale home revolves around a giant-size great room, which includes a living area, dining room, and kitchen. A gigantic Alaskan moose-antler chandelier hangs from the ceiling, supported by log beams thirty-five inches in diameter. Twenty-four-foot-tall windows invite acres and acres of scenic views inside.

Advanced heating methods is the primary technology that has enabled this family and others to transform their one-room-cabin dreams into hand-hewn citadels. With reliable heat, these home owners indulge in large, exposed windows and basketball-court-size rooms with vaulted ceilings, traditionally considered impractical. But the proliferation of these luxurious blue-ribbon log cabins hasn't squelched everyone's longing for an intimate space.

Even the couple in the castle addresses this need. To maintain the feel of a small log cabin, the woman created several intimate spaces beyond the great room: a cave for watching television, a small turret for reading books, balconies with lower ceilings, smaller studies, Swedish bunk beds for her grandchildren, and magical porches. She even moved a one-room soddy onto the property and turned it into a garden teahouse. Within these smaller spaces, occupants relish peace and tranquility so desirable in this rugged country.

As my friend in the toolshed hideaway points out, "A real primitive hideout is not for everyone." But for the romantic, winter in a Rocky Mountain

Many western lodges revolve around great rooms like this. Iron pocket doors designed by Imaging Spence prevent heat from escaping through the chimney when the fireplace isn't in use.

ROCKY MOUNTAIN HOME

cabin provides an enchanting refuge. Edward Abbey once asked himself if the definition of romanticism was the search for the intimate in the remote. Anyone who thrives on the isolation of a snowy day in the mountains would answer in the affirmative.

Four bar stools oversee a small but functional kitchen. Turkish and Greek pots sparkle above the stove.

In this great room, a twenty-one-foot-long, 1920s Yei-Be-Che Navajo rug takes center stage. The moose-antler chandelier was built by John Bickner of Jackson, Wyoming.

The Indian "cigar store"
sculpture is a new one by
F. Gallagher. Inspired by
Swedish design, the bed has
a Navajo rug tucked around
the mattress, and cushions
are made from a mixture
of vintage textiles.

A sculpture of Pan
is a delicate touch in
this massive log home
constructed with recycled
hand-peeled logs.

Visitors to this screened-in garden cabin can enjoy the fresh air down by Fish Creek without the nuisance of bugs.

Wyoming native Lynn Arambel likes to give old things a face-lift. For the garden cabin, she updated pieces of seventies furniture with new upholstery and applied willow.

Arambel likes to work with willow because it is durable and pliable. She applies the willow when it is still a little green. "If treated right, it can be coaxed into so many intricate designs," she says. She creates furniture, birdhouses, and accessories such as picture frames from this abundant Rocky Mountain scrub.

Arambel collects all her own willow. "I like to do the whole job, from cutting the twig to applying the shoots to the furniture. I just feel more connected." Often ranchers invite her to clearcut the willow that grows abundantly in their irrigation ditches. In other locations, she is careful to gather older-looking willows or trimmings from shrubs or trees that are blocking younger plants.

Inspired by the 1917 lodge at the Chief Joseph Ranch in Hamilton, Montana—a prestigious hunting lodge—architect David Leavengood combined stone arches, logs, and cedar shingles to create a home that suits its surroundings.

A painting of Teddy Roosevelt commands attention from the mantel. Upholstered leather couches and chairs provide comfortable seating around the hearth. Details such as an Old Hickory card table, Tiffany lamp, and carved bear (seen in detail photograph) give the room character. "We wanted to create a lodge that felt like it had been here for a hundred years—the feeling of an old lodge with modern conveniences," the owner said.

Sculptor Joffa Kerr spends many hours creating primarily whimsical wildlife bronzes in her Wyoming studio. Old skeletons piled on her shelves provide inspiration.

Many ranches in the Rockies are comprised of a ranch house and several outbuildings, much as old dude ranches were laid out. Instead of piling guests into a main house, ranchers house their guests in small, romantic buildings like this fishing cabin. Both hosts and guests welcome the privacy.

Wildflowers decorate an Old Hickory card table, circa 1940.

89

This writer's office has been
personalized with favorite
accessories, among which is
a gun cabinet by Don
Hindman. Hindman originally
worked for Thomas
Molesworth in the early
1930s, then moved onto
the 63 Dude Ranch, where he
set up a one-man shop.

Log cabins have such a
personal ambience that they
can absorb most types
of collectibles.

In the northern Rockies,
decorators employ primary
colors rather than pastels.
Since winters are often
long and dark, bright reds
help create warm,
cheery environments.

This Montana getaway built
by Terry Baird is simply
a small bedroom. To take a
shower, guests must heat
water over the old stove
inside or over a campfire,
then pour it into an oak
keg that is outfitted with
antique fixtures—and bare
it all outdoors.

This bedroom is in a
basement that was turned
into a rustic den with barn-
wood siding. The walls are
rough gypsum. The lodgepole
bed sweetly bears the
wife's first initial.

The Rocky Mountains have
thousands of spectacular
fishing streams. In keeping
with the spirit of the region,
a minnow bucket makes an
attractive container for wildflowers, while a collection of
Denton fish prints decorates
the wall above a primitive
workbench.

In Keeping

A ONE-EYED COWBOY with a face that matched the granite terrain once took me for a ride in the mountains along with a herd of other dudes. I told him I was an English rider, which along with my wide-brimmed 1920s cowgirl hat and city-slicker confidence seemed to offend him. With a grunt, he boosted me onto my horse, and we set off down the trail.

My horse turned out to be a wild beast with a hard mouth that never once felt the tug of the reins. As we plunged through the river and sailed down steep terrain, I hung on for dear life. At the end of the ride, I slipped off my mount, relieved to feel the ground, humbled by the ride. Inside the tack room, the guide turned to me and, in a slightly less-gruff voice, said, "Not bad for an English rider," and disappeared.

More than any other place I've lived, I've learned that an outsider here has to pay her dues before she can consider herself a local and call this place home. I've yet to discover how many years it takes. Some say after a person has spent a handful of winters here, they earn local respect.

The goal in restoring this 1923 Wyoming log home was to create a period piece. Like many early Wyoming homes, this one has painted wood-plank walls. The floors were also painted and nailed down with hand-cut nails, as they would have been in that era. An eastern white-tailed deer head poses over an early 1900s pie safe.

An older eastern dude rancher told me, however, that "you're a dude till you die."

Since my incident with the cowboy, I've hung up my wide-brimmed hat and tried to curtail my know-it-all behavior. Rather than impose my brazen city ways on this place, I've tried to listen to the country.

In the design business, I have admired those who have done the same. The handful of individuals whose perspectives are represented here are some of the people who have studied the Rockies and, rather than challenge the country, have created designs that are in keeping with the place. Whether a building, an interior space, or a piece of furniture, their works of art reflect native materials and handmade textures. Their designs are respectful of pioneer traditions and reflect a certain modesty of scale. And in all of these projects there is celebration of fine Rocky Mountain craftsmanship.

As more and more people move to the Rocky Mountains, the land and communities are challenged by their needs. Ten-thousand-square-foot houses dominate the mountaintops; outlet stores send mom-and-pop operations out of business; and local caterers have developed healthy businesses supplying sandwiches for private planes that bring the jet set zooming in for a few hours or a few days. As Wallace Stegner wrote in his book *The American West As Living Space*, "Instead of adapting, as we began to do, we have tried to make country and climate over to fit our existing habits and desires."

A 1930s Bengal coal-and-gas stove, "America's Best" by the Floyd-Wells Company, is a romantic and functional addition to this old ranch house. A poker table has been recycled for use in the kitchen by adding a 1920s linoleum covering to match the counters.

The clean white walls
with blue trim provide a
pleasant counterpoint
to the rustic beds.

These burl beds, circa 1920,
were discovered in Montana.
The maker is unknown.
A 1934 painting of the
Pony Express by
H. B. Dunsford commands
the wall space.

No matter how many square feet a home covers, architect Jonathan Foote's projects always begin with simplicity and discretion.

The professionals whose interviews follow believe in turning the tide and are mapping out a viable future. I'd hope that tough old cowboy would approve.

Jonathan L. Foote, Architect

THE FIRST TIME I met Jonathan Foote, we sipped martinis at Stiegler's in Jackson and discussed the debutante's weakness for cowboys. As it turned out, both of us are very fond of these love stories, which are as common in the Rockies as sagebrush.

Every summer, young Foote and his family piled into their station wagon in the East and headed west to summer on a dude ranch. From the corral fence or on some mountain trail, Foote witnessed these delicious East-West *amours* ignite. And he, too, fell in love with the West. "I loved the space," he said, "and here you were judged for what you did, not for who you were."

At the end of our conversation, Foote raced off to meet his plane, wearing his cowboy boots, a silver cutting-horse belt buckle, and an old baseball cap. Soon he would land at home in Livingston, Montana. As I drove back to my cabin, I realized we hadn't even talked about his work. Having previously spent a romantic weekend in one of his architectural creations, I had become a devout fan.

Fortunately, that day was the first of many conversations, and we have since focused on architecture, with an occasional rehashing of the East-meets-West theme.

Since Foote has moved west, he has become one of the most important architects in the Rocky Mountains. His talent seems to have expanded naturally from his boyhood love and respect for the country. In every project, Foote's first commitment is to the land.

The site of this home is an oasis of natural beauty. Moose tromp through the creek, coyotes cruise the pastures, and the sound of birds breaks the silence of the sanctuary. Foote's challenge here was to create a home that didn't intrude on the habitat.

"When invading this scenery with a house, one of the first concerns I have is how it is going to live in that scenery without spoiling it. I wonder, 'How will it find its own being, its own life, in this vast, spectacular place?'"

Before launching into the conception for a new house, Foote tries first to encourage his clients to remodel existing buildings. If there aren't any structures to restore, he uses old hand-hewn logs from barns and homesteads to create buildings with saddle notches and dovetail corners. Although the spaces and shapes are modern, his buildings look and feel as if they have been there a hundred years. His homes, like the brawny sagebrush and the

The owners of this home
wanted Jonathan Foote to
build a structure that
resembled a barn. In this
stylish living room with lofty
ceiling, the walls are made
of barn wood and the
floors are wood.

"This is the most elaborate
mudroom I've ever done,"
Foote says. The clients wanted
a space big enough to throw
their saddles down, store ski
equipment in the closets,
and greet guests. The rustic
table was built by craftsman
James Clair Sharp from
Livingston, Montana.

The residents spend endless hours in this glassed-in porch watching the activity on a rambling creek. Moose, coyote, and deer frequent the area.

snow-fringed pine trees, seem to belong to the Rockies.

Some months after our first rendezvous, Foote returned to Jackson Hole and gave me a tour of his projects there. What I remember most about the afternoon was a particular driveway. Before we started down the dirt road, he told me to imagine I was listening to a symphony. The approach began with a grand view of Glory Peak and the Teton Mountain Range. Then, with the deft motion of a mountain stream, the rutted road meandered past an old buck-and-rail fence, disappeared over a wooden bridge, and darted in and out of gritty old cottonwood trees. Glimpses of a log-and-stone cabin through the woods fueled my curiosity. Unlike many new western homes, this home stood discreetly on its site. Rather than hearing the pompous tuba, I heard a graceful violin.

As we explored the interior, Foote started on one of his passionate soliloquies while I furiously scribbled notes, trying to keep up. "I like simple beginnings, like the beginning of *Moby Dick* . . . the complexity of site is glorified by simple statements. Architecture begins a hundred miles away from a building . . . Architecture is like an opera . . . The design of this home mimics the flow of a river . . .

My favorite book is *Architecture Without Architects . . .*" Just as I managed to squeeze this last bit of information onto the back of my notebook, Foote hurried off to catch his flight.

The detail work of Foote's project architects and craftsmen make his remodeled buildings masterfully authentic. The craftsmen he employs, adept at traditional building methods, use tools such as a broad ax and adze to make dovetail joints like these.

BORN AND RAISED in the East, Foote attended a Massachusetts prep school, then received a B.A. and a master's degree in architecture from Yale University. He practiced his profession full-time in New Haven, Connecticut, and taught architecture as a visiting lecturer at Yale. He was involved in many restoration projects, including two New England towns.

In the seventies, he began to feel restless. Confined by generations of family expectations and feeling cramped creatively, Foote decided to move west. Something in his heart reminded him of dude-ranch days and his boyhood love of the West. "There was a part of me that was validated out there. I was someone I liked being. It was who I really was." So, Foote sold his Connecticut farm in 1974 and closed up his successful architectural firm. He put two cutting horses in the trailer, packed two pairs of Levi's, boots, a couple of shirts, and a denim jacket and headed west. "My heart packed my bag and drove the truck west. I was going to be a cowboy"—a dream he'd harbored since his youth.

For the next few years, Foote traveled the cutting-horse circuit and lived out of a two-room horse trailer. No one had any idea he was an architect; he lived like a cowboy. After two years of riding the circuit, the Montana State University School of Architecture asked him to teach, and Foote entered his profession again but didn't give up his horses.

In 1979, he restored a two-story, red-brick firehouse in Livingston and opened his architectural office inside. Four years later, he opened a second office in Jackson, Wyoming, to meet the demands of clientele there. While Foote still finds time to win silver buckles, he juggles an enormously busy work schedule, building eight to ten major projects a year.

ONE MORNING LAST WINTER, Foote was leaning back in his swivel chair, knitting his bushy brows, trying to describe to Peter Woloszynski and me what inspires him. His son had recently sent him a collection of his drawings from Paris, which were propped up around the room and stacked on the tables. Foote's own bold drawings were tacked on the wall to his left.

"The clients are the most important ingredient. I've got to totally absorb them and understand their views." Once he has sized up their desires and dreams, he wrestles with a design in his head. Usually around three or four in the morning, he rushes down to his

Here the walkway beams become part of the cotton-wood forest.

A moose-antler chandelier glows in the entry. The Bokhara rug, along with western collectibles and hats, are pleasantly playful. An eighteenth-century settle occupies the corner.

With long approaches, Foote creates suspense. The rustic front door, made of eighty-year-old fir, was designed by Foote.

drawing board just off the living room and starts to compose, drawing until his hand stops. "I don't think about drawing, it just comes out. It is so exciting for me to have it come out of my hand. I don't know how it gets out."

Foote's first western project was a result of this mysterious process. His brother had purchased the Meadow Spring Ranch in northern Montana and planned on restoring the habitat and ranching some of the land. Afraid to build on the property for fear a structure might upset the balance of the ecosystem, he called on Jonathan in hopes of a creative solution. From the start, Foote listened to his intuition. "My whole body was coming alive," he said. "This house developed directly from the soul and bypassed the brain."

After walking the property, he sat down on a stump and made a fast and furious sketch. He opted to use an ancient barn as a starting point and incorporate the old homestead buildings found on the ranch into living spaces. By using existing dwellings and old materials, he could create romantic residences that blended with rather than challenged the landscape. "The materials carried with them a certain sense of timelessness."

Foote soon discovered that to make this and other projects work, he needed exceptional craftsmen who had a sensitivity for the old buildings and Montana tradition. Recovered materials are wonderfully rich in history and texture but useless without cautious,

Foote often uses dry-stacked stone as a construction technique. A wooden frame lies between the exterior and interior stone walls.

skilled hands. To ensure success, Foote developed his own construction company, On Site Management. "The irony of it all is that, when recycling the materials, you have to be dead on or else the building looks fake," Foote says. "My craftsmen know you can't just scour a cope. They have to take it slow and make sure they don't blow the splinters. It must come together so it looks natural."

With the precision of a maestro, Foote started out by measuring the quality of a joint with a credit card. If the card couldn't slide through the joint, it was a success. Proof that his craftsmen understand Foote's goal and the spirit of the buildings, they have tossed the credit card and are now using cigarette-rolling paper.

Foote creates the feeling of intimacy in larger buildings by connecting several one-room cabins. Crafted of hand-hewn logs reclaimed from a stage stop, a homestead cabin, and an early 1900s barn, this rustic retreat truly combines past and present.

ONCE I TOLD Foote a ranch romance story that broke my heart. A chore boy named Roy worked for a dude ranch in Big Timber just north of where Foote lives. One summer he fell in love with one of the fancy guests from Boston. Trailing behind him in beautiful, open, rugged country, she believed she loved him too. But when she returned home, she curled her hair and took up with her Brooks Brothers and cotillion crowd again. Memories of summer faded like a dream until one day, Roy appeared at her doorstep.

"What are you doing here?" she asked, obviously surprised.

Despite admonishment from the head of the dude ranch, Roy had quit his ranch job and spent all his earnings on a plane ticket to the

East. Beaming, he said, "You told me you'd love me forever." There was a long silence.

"Oh, Roy, you know I was just kidding." Then she shut the door. Without a penny in his pocket, Roy hitchhiked back to Montana, and the dude rancher gave him his job back.

Sadly, many East-meets-West love affairs end in pools of tears, and the dreams fade like an echo.

Willow benches by Diane Cole provide a quiet spot for respite and observing the goings-on of nature.

JONATHAN FOOTE DEALS in dreams. He builds habitat for romantics like himself. While his clients aren't all easterners and debutantes, they are, for the most part, outsiders who are interested in a Rocky Mountain home for their personal romantic reasons.

It is Foote's job to recognize these fantasies. "As I see it, the practical world doesn't give us a lot of opportunity for indulging in our fantasies. A life without fantasy is pretty limited and becomes humdrum," he says. "The West is a place where people can work right next to a stream where they catch their dream trout—or at least go after it—a place where they can take two hours out of a work day to ski in four feet of fresh powder. The West is a place where their true romantic spirit can be nurtured and can reach

An Early American quilt covers an antique walnut Venetian bed in the master bedroom.

A hearty hand-hewn door leads into a Foote home.

This twelve-room lodge is set
amid cottonwood trees near
snowcapped Glory Peak in
the Teton Mountain Range.

heights they never imagined existed. I think the idea of the West has carried a fantasy with it, but the process of how one gets involved in the West can either reinforce the place or snuff it out."

Foote, with his team of architects and craftsmen, offers a viable path. He won't build a cowboy castle arrogantly placed on a butte. Instead, he connects several one-room cabins to maintain a modest, unassuming scale inside and outside. "The area is so beautiful and overwhelms me in so many different ways, that it astounds me that we have to resort to exaggeration." There are other ways to contribute to the continuation and preservation of the West our hearts first fluttered for.

"For people coming from a different place, it is important to make a graceful entry. People have a responsibility to tread lightly, to observe tribal customs and take a back seat."

Foote's houses of old logs, reused siding, stone, and stucco are proof that he is true to his word. "This place belongs here," he says, describing one of his buildings. "It's not an imitation of something in the past. It has its own life in the twentieth century, but it respects a thousand years before and a thousand years yet to come."

A snowy road passes through a wooded area and arrives at this private sanctuary. Originally a Montana homestead, this cabin was moved to Wyoming and remodeled for a permanent residence.

A magnificent truss turns heads toward the ceiling in this Foote home.

Hilary Heminway on Western Design

DESIGNING AN INTERIOR in the Rocky Mountains presents a number of challenges. Most mountain towns don't support a variety of designer showrooms; general stores don't carry Brunschwig & Fils; and the upholsterer usually lives some eight hours down the highway or only does tractor seats. The alternative is usually custom work, which, while well worth the wait, takes time.

One of Heminway's design trademarks is finding new uses for old junk. Here spoons work as fun and informal kitchen-cabinet handles.

Then, there are other routine obstacles. Someone builds a house on a mountaintop, where a moving van or U-Haul can't ascend. Or a furniture maker creates a wonderful sturdy lodgepole bed that doesn't fit through the front door, so it has to be mounted on a forklift and lowered through the roof.

Designer Hilary Heminway, who splits her time between the East Coast and the Rockies, understands the rigors of Rocky Mountain design. She encourages her clients to wait for a handcrafted piece. She will drive across the prairie in a snowstorm to tell the upholsterer exactly how the chair should be done. She also has the savvy to suggest postponing the purchase of a ten-thousand-dollar couch if what her client really needs is a new truck or tractor for the ranch.

Although small, this kitchen is functional. The room features two Old Hickory bar stools, a primitive cowboy chair, and an old wood-burning stove. To shed light on the cooking area, Heminway turned a junk-store coffee grinder into a lamp.

Heminway's cabin overlooks
the Boulder River.

The lodgepole couches—
designed by Hilary Heminway
and built by Ken Siggins of
Triangle Z Ranch Furniture—
furnish the living room. By
combining the light fixtures
with the couch, Heminway
eliminated extra tables that
would have cluttered this
small room. A primitive
Montana cowboy chair is in
the foreground.

Besides common sense, Heminway has a natural flair for the hand-hewn style. As a child, like Jonathan Foote, she was introduced to the Rocky Mountains at a dude ranch, where, twenty years later, she proceeded to fall in love with a cowboy because "he knew all the names of the wildflowers and took me places I'd never seen."

In the 1970s, her family purchased a cattle ranch and a fishing camp in Montana. Rather than imitate fashion, Heminway creates interiors she believes suit the lifestyle. "I just follow my instincts," she says.

The netting allows Heminway to read at night without the bother of moths.

For Heminway, the most important element of western design is comfort. "Cowboys would never sit in a saddle that was uncomfortable for ten hours a day, so why would they want to come into a cabin and sit in a place that wasn't comfortable?" Furniture, layout, and lighting have to be functional. A home has to be designed to live in.

"I always want to feel that I can read a book anyplace, whether it be in the dining room or the kitchen. There has to be good enough light to read a book," she says. "I also want to feel comfortable eating anywhere—also romancing anywhere. So, I always put dimmers on lights in the kitchen and bathrooms. Who would want to make love in the kitchen with stainless steel and the lights blaring?"

One way to achieve comfort is to create the proper scale. Walking into Heminway's family-owned Bar 20 Ranch, a former

Behind the Victorian oak dining table is an old chair from Montana's OT Ranch. The chair, favored by regular guest Teddy Roosevelt, was reupholstered in leather and fringe.

This three-little-bears room is for Heminway's children. The beds were built by Indy Corson. Posters by contemporary western artist Buckeye Blake hang above the bed.

1920s dude ranch, one immediately feels at home. The old ranch house is one story, the ceilings are low, and the rooms are small. "There were very few two-story houses out West historically, and that was for a good reason. One-story houses stayed cool in the summer and warm in the winter. Pioneers also didn't have the machinery to get those logs up higher than they could reach." As in most primitive buildings, it is the human scale that gives the Bar 20 an enchanting warmth.

Heminway uses humor in her ranch and most of her other projects to enhance the informal ambience. "I guess I just grew up in a household that played practical jokes all the time. I think people take their houses too seriously. I want people to laugh in my houses. It is a relief for the eye and the heart. Humor also makes a house comfortable and unpretentious." Hilary once had a relative who used to burst out laughing listening to a symphony. "I think in decorating, one should relieve the eye as one relieves the ear with humor. It might not be something that people would pick up on just like that. It could be done with color. It could be done with scale. I placed a beautiful French Louis chair and put a little twig table next to it. This was a combination that to me was humorous. I like to wonder who once sat in that period chair and what would they think of this Adirondack table. Somehow it is connected historically—French fur trappers—but not visually; yet, perhaps they are connected visually."

An unsigned oil painting of fish positioned over an old dry sink makes a stark but refined statement.

By recycling materials and objects, Heminway gives her interiors a history and connects them to tradition. "I love turning something that is just sitting there into something someone can use." She delights in turning an egg incubator into a coffee table, a circa-1900 coffee grinder into a kitchen lamp, and a formal gigantic wing chair once favored by Teddy Roosevelt into a leather western seat with fringed leather antimacassars. These pieces have a past, and their textures and stories link the users to the past.

Heminway's latest recycling project has been revamping old sheep wagons into a veritable collection of luxurious retreats. "Everyone these days has portable phones, portable computers. I wanted a portable office."

Before Heminway even had a chance to build her office, she had a request for a guest room. Since this first one, she and her partner, Terry Baird, a Montana craftsman committed to historic cabin restoration and new construction, have solidified their business, Montana Wagons. Sheep wagons can be electrified, plumbed, telephoned, faxed, flushed, cooked, cooled, heated, and TVed. And their uses are endless: workshop, love nest, doghouse, playhouse, kitchen, studio, in-law apartment, chapel, ranch museum, caretaker's cabin, hot-dog stand, and snore-a-torium.

This guest bathroom shows off the western style's funky side. On the right-hand side of the sink is a bubble gum wrapper that Heminway found in her Teddy Roosevelt chair.

"It's fun to take something that had a useful life, something that most people would just burn, and all of a sudden have something people like," Baird says.

In the past and still today, sheepherders lived in these 7-by-12-foot wagons out on the range with usually only a dog, a horse, and flock of sheep. The wagon was their house. Although the quarters were tight, they had all they needed. And when the bands moved, they hitched their horse to their house and followed.

While Montana Wagons are more fashionable than the early ones, they still provide "an inhabitant with all they need." Like a tent, a small cabin, a tree house, a lighthouse, these small, primitive hideouts inspire retreat. And the wagon, like Heminway's small dude-ranch cabin, has a human scale that invites you inside and promises comfort, safety, and solace.

CREATING AN INTIMATE AND informal style in a larger shelter takes more than a comfortable couch, lights on dimmers, and a sense of humor, Heminway admits. The very nature of a giant structure challenges the intimacy and practicality of a smaller place.

Before beginning a larger project, Heminway always warns her clients about the pitfalls of a large log home. "The thing that is the hardest for me to convince clients of is the enormity of the upkeep in these places." Dead flies accumulate in the windows; spider webs and layers of dust abound in the nooks and crannies. The ambience in these larger spaces fringed with floor-to-ceiling windows also can be more daunting than the mountain landscape. Basketball-court-sized living rooms—furnished with couches and chairs that look like they were stolen from the set of *The Incredible Shrinking Woman*—defy a comfortable human scale.

But, as Heminway and one client proved, comfort can be achieved in a lodge-sized home such as Montana's Corral Creek. "The challenge I face in a larger home is to be able to put a couch in a room and make it look like it belongs there. Also, when a person sits on the couch, he or she should feel like a part of the room." To achieve this desirable intimacy, Hilary varies fabric textures and juxtaposes furniture of different heights, styles, and mass. "Having everything at the same height is a no-no, and so I try to wave the room like an ocean, or the mountains, or like the prairie, which even in its flatness gives you a sense of ups and downs." She knows she has succeeded when someone remarks, "This house is so big, but it feels so inviting."

The wagon is an adult playhouse, a delightful alternative to staying in the main lodge a few minutes' walk away.

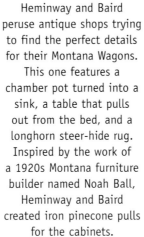

Heminway and Baird peruse antique shops trying to find the perfect details for their Montana Wagons. This one features a chamber pot turned into a sink, a table that pulls out from the bed, and a longhorn steer-hide rug. Inspired by the work of a 1920s Montana furniture builder named Noah Ball, Heminway and Baird created iron pinecone pulls for the cabinets.

Corral Creek: A Model for Rocky Mountain Tradition

A PLEASING NEW Rocky Mountain home often depends on a collaboration of talent. At Montana's Corral Creek ranch, a number of people—the owners, architects, contractors, craftsmen, and interior designer—worked together to create a romantic retreat.

The project began with a couple's dream of owning a cattle ranch situated in a remote area but near a small cowboy town. After a ten-year search, they discovered an ideal property in the Madison Valley of Montana, on the outskirts of West Yellowstone. The place was private and adjacent to blue-ribbon trout streams. Wild animals roamed in the backyard and land was open for grazing cattle. A small western town lay a short jaunt down a country road. Several old ranch buildings stood on the property, but the structures were uninhabitable, so the couple looked into building a lodge from scratch.

Drawings by architects David Leavengood of Seattle, Washington, and later by Larry Pearson of Rollins, Montana, provided a start. As the building evolved, the contractor on the job—Yellowstone Traditions of Bozeman, Montana—played a significant role in shaping the lodge into a unique, hand-hewn retreat.

"The owners came to us with a vision and a feel, and it was our job to interpret," says Harry Howard of Yellowstone Traditions.

"Harry was so full of ideas," said one of the owners. "It was like letting a wild stallion loose and being on his back with no reins."

The logs used to build this home were collected from two drainages in Montana's Madison Valley. They had been beetle-killed or were deadfall from a fire. A unique corner seat and an antique carved bear spruce up this alcove under the stairway.

Oversized couches sit side
by side with leather
armchairs by Jimmy and
Lynda Covert. The fireplace
was crafted with indigenous
materials by stonemason
Phil Cox. The upstairs
banister features lodgepole
from the property.

A mosaic sideboard hand-
crafted by Jimmy Covert
from juniper, cherry, and
assorted driftwood welcomes
guests into the foyer.
A similar piece by Covert
won the Buffalo Bill Historical
Center's Switchback Ranch
Purchase Award in 1994 and
resides in the museum.
A Black Forest antique bear
makes a handy hat rack.

Lodgepole beds designed by
Hilary Heminway and built
by Ken Siggins of Triangle
Z Ranch Furniture decorate
the children's room.
A western toy box adds a
contemporary touch.

Inspired by the classic style
of national park lodges such
as Old Faithful Inn, this
home centers around a great
room. All the mica shades
and rawhide details were
created by Bob Blanchet of
Dubois, Wyoming.

A handcrafted mailbox mimics the Rocky Mountain pioneer style.

The kitchen table is made from a rustic door from Mexico. Chairs that pull the room together in the Rocky Mountain ranch tradition are by New West of Cody.

In the tradition of Lake McDonald Lodge at Glacier National Park, Yellowstone Traditions used two western red cedar trunks, cut from a private reserve in northern Idaho, to frame the front door of the Corral Creek Lodge. Red cedar is rot resistant, holds its bark well, and is aromatic. Wood reclaimed from a hand-hewn cabin makes up the front door.

With extensive experience in restoring old park buildings and ranches, Yellowstone Traditions sought to emulate a native style. "Much of the house was built intuitively," Howard says. The company used hand-hewn wood from primitive buildings and local deadfall lodgepole pine and stone. Local craftsmen worked forging iron, laying stone, saddle notching timbers, and building furniture. Red cedar trunks frame the front entrance like they do at Glacier National Park's McDonald Lodge, and the rustic banister that fringes the great room mimics the timeless banister in the Old Faithful Inn.

From the beginning, Hilary Heminway was part of the team to help create a western interior. The owners wanted "a place that looked warm and inviting but didn't look like it was decorated—a place where people could put their feet up and feel at home."

Heminway mixed and matched locally handcrafted furniture with antiques and lighter pieces with serious works of art to create comfortable textures and spaces. But as everyone on the project says, the place succeeds as a result of a blend of talents. "The project became more of a canvas for everyone than a job," the owners said.

T. Baird Construction

IN 1922, Clarence Farnsworth built a
16-by-22-foot cabin for his bride-to-be in
Montana's Boulder Valley. With the utmost
care, he hand hewed his logs and connected
them with a dovetail notch. Then he laid a
fir floor, built some furnishings, and hoped
he'd find a companion. Upon meeting one
girl, he told her he loved her and wanted
to marry her. As the story goes, she screamed and ran away. Sadly,
Farnsworth never did marry, but he was hopeful to the end.

Instead of installing just an outdoor faucet, Baird opted to create an outdoor sink for washing up in the summer, or perhaps for cleaning a fish. A galvanized tin sink with drain board rests in a barn-wood frame.

    On his deathbed, Mr. Farnsworth was politely asked by a good
neighbor if he could buy his land. "I'll tell you what," Farnsworth
said. "If I don't get married, you can buy the place."

    This is just one of many stories that inspires Terry Baird, a
Montana builder with a passion and intuitive sense for restoring old
cabins. "I like making a silk purse out of a sow's ear," he says.
Farnsworth's cabin was just this kind of project.

    Baird purchased the old place from Farnsworth's neighbor. As
in most cases, the neighbor was happy to get rid of it. His other
option was to burn the cabin down to eliminate taxable property.

An electrified kerosene
lantern now illuminates this
remodeled cabin.

Many owners just want to
burn down these homestead
cabins, but Terry Baird buys
dilapidated structures such
as these and turns them into
intimate getaways.

A porch is a simple
addition that not only
adds to the charm of an
old place but makes the
home seem larger.

In this bedroom—an
upstairs addition to a homestead cabin constructed by
Terry Baird—Kent Interiors
of Bozeman, Montana,
wanted to give the new
room the same ambience as
the decades-old original
building. A vintage iron bed
and an old trunk for linen
storage help accomplish
the goal.

Although weathered and rickety, Baird knew he could turn the aging dwelling into a unique retreat.

Baird remodeled the cabin for a client who lives a crow's flight away from the original homestead. After numbering the logs, dismantling the cabin, and moving the pieces onto its new site, Baird built a foundation, then reconstructed the cabin with synthetic chinking, using the familiar dovetail notch. Inside, he laid down the original flooring and replaced the ladder to the second floor with a staircase. Upstairs he added a dormer to give the bedroom a little more space, and outside he built a porch. Of course, he installed electricity and plumbing. Even with these modern alterations, the cabin still stands with dignity.

Baird credits the success of his projects to the expertise and patience of his crew. "Many people think new is good and old is bad," he says. "Number one, I have to find carpenters who don't mind picking up an old board and pounding nails out of it and making something of it. Some carpenters just absolutely will not."

As we drove away from the old pioneer cabin, bumping along a dirt road, Baird wondered if Farnsworth—who had put so much blood, sweat, and tears into the place—would approve of his work. "I wonder if he could see it if he would be happy with what I did. I don't know. I would hope so."

It is Baird's respect for the history of these old buildings and their creators that allows him to preserve their souls.

This 1900s Montana cabin, like many others in the state, was originally built by a Scandinavian immigrant. The logs were hauled from East Boulder's Green Mountain with a team of horses. Typical of the Swedish style predominant in the region, the builder used hand-hewn logs and dovetail joints. Terry Baird restored this cabin and added a second floor, giving the home a striking contemporary appearance while keeping with the spirit of the original homestead.

Montana builder Terry Baird lives in a log cabin because it makes sense. "You don't have to worry about painting it, and the rustic furniture can withstand the dog," he says. If you want to drive a nail to hang a picture, you get a sixteenth penny and pound it in there, and when you're done you jerk it out of the wall and it enhances the look of the thing. You do that to a Sheetrock house or you move a nice piece of furniture into a house and you scratch it, you ruin the whole thing."

Bringing the piece of aged driftwood onto the deck is an ingenious way to blend the home and the environment. Baird's Airedale watches the East Boulder River flow by their home. In the summer, the river is so loud that it becomes an audible part of their environment indoors as well as out.

Baird added a second floor
to this Montana homestead
and rechinked the cabin
with a synthetic chinking,
Sashco's log jam. The double-
hung windows with true
divided light were typical of
traditional windows used in
the early part of this century.
These, however, feature
thermal panes.

An outdoor porch on
this primitive cabin invites
relaxation.

A buffalo head surrounded
by precious antiques
and junk-store finds give the
Mangy Moose in Jackson,
Wyoming, an authentic
ambience of the Rocky
Mountain West.

A rare Greene and Greene
door blends comfortably with
the western decor. A milk
wagon full of Indian textiles
is on the left. A framed
Charlie Russell letter leans
against the window, and
the shelves below display
Indian baskets. A Navajo
olla rests on the bench.

Pillows trimmed in rope
and an antler lamp add a
simple western touch to
this bedroom.

A collection of paintings
by artist Russell Chatham
are high on display
in this traditional-style
Montana home.

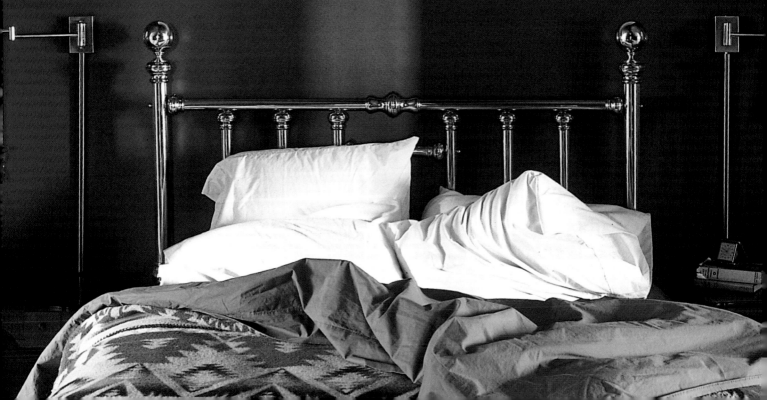

This iron porch railing depicts cowboys involved in various activities—rounding up cattle, branding, and gathering around a chuck wagon. There couldn't be a more ideal backdrop for this work of art than the mountains in Wapiti, Wyoming. The metalwork is by Miller Metal Studios in Cody.

Bill Schenck's serigraph gives this boy's room a pop-western twist.

One of Jimmy Covert's
earliest driftwood desks
is a pleasing reminder of
the rugged Northwest
in this Southwest-style
guest room designed
by Cabin Creek Designs.
An L. D. Burke mirror
leans against the wall.

Molesworth-style furniture
created by Lester Santos of
Cody furnishes this home.
The home was designed
by architect Jonathan Foote
and decorated by Cabin
Creek Designs.

Rough-sawn barn-wood
walls give this room
a rustic feeling. A ladder
leads to a loft.

Jordan of Jackson, Wyoming, created this fine hand-forged fire screen and set of fire tools. "I'd wanted to live out West since I was a boy," Jordan says. "The cowboy hat I wear was from a friend named Tex, who could swing a twenty-foot bullwhip and cut a cigarette hanging from a person's mouth in half." By merging his talent with his passion for the West, Jordan creates one-of-a-kind pieces of metal art. His love of the style has even prompted him to do some metal restoration work at Yellowstone's Old Faithful Inn, gratis.

A rustic table and a hat
rack built by James Clair
Sharp stand in the middle
of this entry hall. Aspen
branches make an attractive
centerpiece.

An Indian totem guards a
river-rock shower.

Early rodeo postcards inside
a vintage frame make
an attractive wall hanging.

Epilogue

ON MY WAY HOME from Montana last year, I stopped in an antique shop, hoping to find a small souvenir. After sifting through rooms full of multicolored glassware, rustic furniture, crocheted blankets, and kitschy cowboy-boot salt-'n'-pepper shakers, I spotted a small, six-dollar, glass oil lamp. It was the perfect treasure.

Back home, I borrowed oil and a wick from a friend and received instructions on how to work my old-fashioned light. After sunset, I lit the wick, placed the glass lantern over the flame, and, as I had been told to do, cranked the fire down with the small metal knob. Then I took the lamp into my darkened bedroom and watched yellow light flicker over the log walls.

I was delighted to discover that, on this snowy evening, I could read passages from a favorite book under the amber glow much like an old cowboy or ranch woman would have done some hundred years ago.

Ever since I've lived in the Rockies, I've relished connections with the past. Hand-hewn homestead cabins or a six-dollar lamp tell stories about a rugged frontier life that has shaped our nation's character.

Tack and a few cowboy collectibles have accumulated in the entrance to a 1923 ranch house.

Because my great-great-grandfather ventured west in the 1840s, I'm fascinated by tales of hearty, self-reliant characters exploring this wild country. Although my life is luxurious compared to my ancestors', splitting wood, warming by a wood-burning stove, or just lighting an old-fashioned lamp feeds my romantic imagination.

But much more than the tools and artifacts of pioneer life, connections to the land also provide perspective. Furniture maker Diane Cole says she moved to Montana to live outdoors. By collecting willows and building rustic furniture, she stays connected to the natural world. "When the world seems so technical and out of control, getting close to the natural world is really a peaceful way to gain perspective."

Artisan Jimmy Covert once said that a true Rocky Mountain shelter is just a protective shell. "Actually, you're trying to live outdoors."

And as one of my dearest friends and mentor pointed out, we live in a place where the views are much more important than the style of bathroom fixtures. As in the past, the drama and beauty of the mountains and the space just outside the front door inspires courage, hope, and possibility.

Of course, I did find out why old-timers don't live in cabins anymore—they are freezing cold. On a winter morning, I reluctantly leave my warm comforter and immediately don my one-piece long underwear, parka, and sometimes ski hat. I wear this outfit until I can get a good fire burning in the stove.

Although ranching is becoming more difficult to sustain out West, it is still an important western industry and one that determined people are striving to preserve in the Rockies.

This traditional country style—a red picket-fence bed, an old quilt, and a flag—works well in a western home.

An old ship lamp hangs
off the dining room of the
Mangy Moose, decorated
with western memorabilia
and colorful Americana.

In the 1920s, travelers between Pinedale and Jackson, Wyoming, stopped here to rest. Today, furniture maker Roy Fisk lives here with his wife Carolyn. Fisk builds exquisite handmade furniture in the dining room.

Cabins can also be dark and gloomy in the thick of winter. Eventually the lack of light prompts an uncomfortable spell of cabin fever. Cobwebs breed in every nook and cranny and spiders love my tub.

Sometimes when I spend an evening grooming my cabin interior with a feather duster, I wonder why on earth I bother to reside in such a primitive building. But living in a Rocky Mountain cabin—for all its challenges and adaptations of lifestyle—has, for me, been worthwhile for the connections it provides to the past and for the adventure of living on the frontier.

Cowboy dealer Brian Lebel
of Old West Antiques likes
everything old. When some
early cabins came up for sale
at the Valley Ranch, where
he had once worked,
he hurried to the sale and
purchased these two guest
cabins. They were small
enough to load onto a
flatbed trailer. They now sit
on his property in Wapiti,
Wyoming, and his guests get
to spend summer nights
tucked away in these
restored buildings, imagining
how the early travelers in
this area near Yellowstone
might have felt.

Acknowledgments

THANK YOU TO all the homeowners who graciously invited us into their homes. We also appreciated help from Beyond Necessity, Old West Antiques, The Back Porch, Becker Gallery, Showcase Antiques, Fighting Bear Antiques, and the Mangy Moose.

Jimmy and Lynda Covert, Lynn Arambel, Diane Cole, Hilary Heminway, Terry and Jill Baird, and Carol Andrews spoiled us with their enthusiasm and support. Jonathan Foote's leadership and passion for the subject was invaluable.

Thanks also to Flowers by Cecelia for all the arrangements, and to Jackson Hole Custom Color Lab for developing our film at a moment's notice. We are grateful to editors Madge Baird and Caroll Shreeve for their expert guidance and to designer Kathleen Timmerman for capturing the mood.

Finally, thanks to my mom and sisters, and especially my dad, who generously provided me with my own precious writing hideout —the shed.

Sources

Preface

Page 10: **Old Hickory rocker and Thomas Molesworth club chair** from Fighting Bear Antiques, P.O. Box 3812, 35 E. Simpson, Jackson, WY 83001, 307-733-2669.

Page 11: **Bathroom accessories** from The Back Porch, P.O. Box 2887, 145 E. Pearl Ave., Jackson, WY 83001, 307-733-0030.

Page 12: **Vintage cowboy clothing** from Old West Antiques, 1215 Sheridan Ave., Cody, WY 82414, 307-587-9014.

Page 13: **Hickory chairs** from Fighting Bear Antiques. **Country cabinet** from Beyond Necessity Antiques & Folk Arts, P.O. Box 779, 335 S. Millward, Jackson, WY 83001, 307-733-7492. **Texas bench** from Milo Marks Furniture, P.O. Box 208, Hwy 6, Meridian, TX 76665, 817-435-2173.

Page 19: **Molesworth lamp** from Fighting Bear Antiques.

Page 20: **Arts & Crafts candlesticks** from United Crafts, 127 W. Putnam Ave., Suite 123, Greenwich, CT 06830, 203-869-4898.

A Pioneer Style

Page 22: **Yard-long vintage photograph** from Old West Antiques, 1215 Sheridan Ave., Cody, WY 82414, 307-587-9014.

Page 32: **Cream cans** from Fighting Bear Antiques, P.O. Box 3812, 35 E. Simpson, Jackson, WY 83001, 307-733-2669.

Pages 36–37: **1920s Two Grey Hills rug** and **buffalo skull** from Fighting Bear Antiques. **Tramp art box** from Showcase Antiques, P.O. Box 82, 115 E. Broadway, Jackson, WY 83001, 307-733-4848.

Snowbound

Page 41: **French doors** by Pella, 1-800-54-PELLA.

Page 42: **Charlie Dye drawing** from Trailside Americana Fine Art Galleries, P.O. Box 1149, 105 Center St., Jackson, WY 83001, 307-733-3186.

Page 46: **Clyde Anderson furniture** and **Navajo rug** from Fighting Bear Antiques, P.O. Box 3812, 35 E. Simpson, Jackson, WY 83001, 307-733-2669.

Page 48: **Chandelier** made by Mike Wilson of Big Horn Antler Furniture & Design, P.O. Box 306, Jackson, WY 83001, 307-733-3491. **Ticking blanket** from Old West Antiques, 1215 Sheridan Ave., Cody, WY 82414, 307-587-9014.

Page 49: **Sculptured chair** by John Mortensen of The Rainbow Trail Collection, P.O. Box 746, Wilson, WY 83014, 307-733-1519.

Page 52: **Pendleton blankets** from Jackson Hole Pendleton Shop, Box 3378, 60 E. Broadway, Jackson, WY 83001, 800-835-6582.

Page 57: **Germantown blanket** from Becker Gallery, 155 Center St., P.O. Box 1144, Jackson, WY 83001, 307-733-1331. **Weather vane** from Auth Antiques, 2543 Fullum, Montreal, Quebec H2K 3P5, 514-526-9765.

Page 58: **Table and chairs** from Cabbage Rose, 307-587-2750, or contact Whispering Pines Antiques, 12 S. Broadway, Red Lodge, MT 59068, 406-446-1470. **Cabinet** from Auth Antiques.

Page 59: ***Buffet a deux corts*** from Auth Antiques.

Page 64: Bottom right photo, **Molesworth chair and rustic floor lamp** from Fighting Bear Antiques. **Interior design** by Astrid Sommer, 3742 Washington St., San Francisco, CA 94118.

Page 65: **Builder Michael Beauchemin** of Beauchemin Construction & Crane Services Inc., P.O. Box 1316, Jackson, WY 83001, 307-733-7640.

Hideouts

Page 69: **Leavengood Architects**, 506 Second Ave., Suite 1922, Seattle, WA 98104, 206-382-1694.

Page 70: **Bed and hat rack** by Diane Cole of Rustic Furniture, 10 Cloninger Lane, Bozeman, MT 59715, 406-586-3746. **Stonework** by Phillip B. Cox of Big Sky Masonry, 308 Prairie Ave., Bozeman, MT 59715, 406-585-1231 or 406-682-7863. **Fire screen** by George Ainslie of Prairie Elk Forge, 202 First Ave. E., P.O. Box 234, Lavina, MT 59046, 406-636-2391.

Page 75: **Outside table** by Jimmy Covert, 907 Canyon Ave., Cody, WY 82414, 307-527-6761.

Pages 76–77: **Mixed media work by artist Greta Gretzinger** available at Barney Wyckoff Gallery, 312 E. Hyman Ave., Aspen, CO 81612, 970-925-8274, or contact Gretzinger, P.O. Box 822, Wilson, WY 83014, 307-733-1389.

Pages 78–83: **Yei-Be-Che Navajo** from Fighting Bear Antiques, P.O. Box 3812, 35 E. Simpson, Jackson, WY 83001, 307-733-2669. **Chandelier** from John Bickner of Elkhorn Industries, P.O. Box 234, 36 E. Broadway, Jackson, WY 83001, 307-733-3916. **Interior design** by Spence Collections, P.O. Box 548, Jackson, WY 83001.

Pages 84–85: **Lynn Sedar Arambel** of Ranch Willow Furniture Co. and Design Studio, 501 U.S. Hwy 14, Sheridan, WY 82801, 307-674-1510.

Page 86: **Sculptures** by Joffa Kerr, P.O. Box 25106, Jackson, WY 83001, 307-733-8829.

Page 87: **Upholstered chair and couch** from National Upholstering Company, 4000 Adeline St., Oakland, CA 94608, 510-653-8915. **Old Hickory card table** from Fighting Bear Antiques. Leavengood Architects.

Page 88: **Flowers by Cecelia**, P.O. Box 8825, Jackson, WY 83002, 307-733-0423.

Page 91: **Wagon wheel couch**, circa 1950, **Molesworth club chair,** and **vintage spurs** from Fighting Bear Antiques.

In Keeping

Page 96: **Vintage linoleum** from 1920s–1950 available at Second Hand Rose, 270 Lafayette St., New York, NY 10012, 212-431-7673.

Jonathan Foote

Pages 98–111: **Jonathan Foote**, 126 E. Callender, Livingston, MT 59047, 406-222-6866.

Page 100: **James Clair Sharp,** 723 N. Yellowstone, Livingston, MT 59047, 406-222-9681.

Page 105: **Chandelier** by Elkhorn Designs, P.O. Box 7663, 70 S. Cache St., Jackson, WY 83001, 307-733-4655.

Page 109: **Benches**—one by James Clair Sharp, others by Diane Cole of Rustic Furniture, 10 Cloninger Lane, Bozeman, MT 59715, 406-586-3746.

Hilary Heminway

Pages 112–19: **Hilary Heminway Interiors,** 140 Briarpatch Rd., Stonington, CT 06378, 860-535-3110 or 406-932-4350.

Page 112: **Old Hickory Furniture Company,** 403 S. Noble St., Shelbyville, IN 46176, 800-232-BARK.

Page 114: **Triangle Z Ranch Furniture,** P.O. Box 995, Cody, WY 82414, 307-587-3901.

Page 116: **Indy Corson of Lupine Log Arts,** 13750 Kelly Canyon Rd., Bozeman, MT 59715, 406-587-0672. **Buckeye Blake art** available at the Big Horn Gallery, 1167 Sheridan Ave., Cody, WY 82414, 307-527-7587.

Pages 122–23: **Montana Wagons,** Box 1, McLeod, MT 59052, 406-932-4350 or 203-535-3110.

Corral Creek

Pages 124–28: **Leavengood Architects,** 506 Second Ave., Suite 1922, Seattle, WA 98104, 206-382-1694. **Larry Pearson, Architect,** P.O. Box 231, Rollins, MT 59931, 406-844-2489. **Yellowstone Traditions** owned by Harry Howard & Dennis Derham, Box 1933, Bozeman, MT 59771, 406-587-0968. **Hilary Heminway Interiors,** 140 Briar Patch Rd., Stonington, CT 06378, 860-535-3110 or 406-932-4350. **Big Sky Masonry,** 308 Prairie Ave., Bozeman, MT 59715, 406-585-1231. **Jimmy and Lynda Covert,** 907 Canyon Ave., Cody, WY 82414, 307-527-6761. **Triangle Z Ranch Furniture,** P.O. Box 995, Cody, WY 82414, 307-587-3901. **Bob Blanchet,** P.O. Box 4, Dubois, WY 82513, 307-455-2568. **Mike and Virginia Patrick of New West,** 2811 Big Horn Ave., Cody, WY 82414, 307-587-2839.

T. Baird Construction

Pages 129–35: **T. Baird Construction,** Box 3, Big Timber, MT 59011, 406-932-6116.

Page 131: **Kent Interiors,** 533 E. Mendenhall, Bozeman, MT 59715, 406-587-8900.

Page 136: **The Mangy Moose,** Teton Village, WY 83025, 307-733-4913.

Page 139: **Chatham Fine Art,** 120 N. Main, Livingston, MT 59047, 406-222-1566.

Page 140: **Bill Schenck,** summer, P.O. Box 47, Moran, WY 83013, 307-543-2302; winter, 5726 E. Forest St., Apache Junction, AZ 85219, 602-982-0086/602-982-4105.

Page 141: **Miller Metal Studios,** 612 Diamond Basin Rd., Cody, WY 82414, 307-527-6687.

Page 142: **Cabin Creek Designs,** P.O. Box 25118, Jackson, WY 83001, 307-733-0274. **Lester Santos of Arcadia Woodworks,** 2208 Public St., Cody, WY 82414, 307-587-6543.

Page 143: **Jimmy Covert,** 907 Canyon Ave., Cody, WY 82414, 307-527-6761. **L.D. Burke,** 1516 Pacheco St., Santa Fe, NM 87505, 505-986-1866, 505-983-8001.

Page 145: **Jordan Metal Works,** 4050 S. Hwy 89, P.O. Box 3285, Jackson, WY 83001, 307-739-2210.

Page 146: **James Clair Sharp,** 723 N. Yellowstone, Livingston, MT 59047, 406-222-9681.

Old things connect us to
our past and, for this reason
alone, are worth saving.